ROOM
for CHANGE

Published by Revival Publishing
Austin, Texas
www.revivalredesign.com

For ordering information or special discounts for bulk purchases, please contact
E. Strong at 123 Battery Way, Peachtree City, GA, 30269, 678.364.1881

Design and composition by Greenleaf Book Group LLC

Cover design by Greenleaf Book Group LLC
Illustrations by David Austin Clar and Benjamin Reece

Cataloging-in-Publication data

Publisher's Cataloging-in-Publication Data (Prepared by the Donohue Group, Inc.)

Reynolds, Susan W.
   Room for change : practical ideas for reviving after
loss / Susan W. Reynolds. -- 1st ed.

   p. : ill. ; cm.

   ISBN: 978-1-4515241-2-3

1. Loss (Psychology) 2. Adjustment (Psychology) 3. Bereavement--
Psychological aspects. 4. Interior decoration--Psychological aspects. I. Title.

BF575.D35 R49 2010
155.9/37

Printed in the United States of America on acid-free paper

First Edition

ROOM
for CHANGE

Practical Ideas
for Reviving After Loss

Susan W. Reynolds

Revival Publishing

Contents

Dedication

This book is dedicated to:

Alice Strong, my mom, for nurturing me and nurturing my concept of home

Peggie Munson, my friend and hospice nurse, for listening and helping me take my first steps through grief

Ann Anderson, my friend and instructor, for teaching me redesign and teaching me compassion for myself

Sarah Holdaway and Christin Reynolds, my friends and my daughters, for supporting me in my changes

Les Morgan, my friend and writing mentor, for watering the seeds for this project. My first blog was inspired by him, a stranger, answering the phone on the first day of spring 2009. He simply said, "Start blogging," and I responded, "What is blogging?" I used the blogs I wrote as the basis for this book. You never know what doors will open. I am blessed.

Preface

When you break a bone, you visit an orthopedic surgeon and receive rehabilitation with a physical therapist.

When your heart has an irregular beat, your visit to the cardiologist may include a combination of medication, surgery and cardiac rehabilitation.

When your heart is broken from a loss, be it the loss of a job, loss of status, loss of partner or spouse, loss of child or loss of dreams, where do you go?

With all of the above you return home to your haven.

With your leg in a cast and mobility limited, you might move a chair or change the position of the bed. With cardiac limitations, you may use a downstairs bedroom for a while rather than climbing the stairs to your old bedroom. You decrease the burdens and obstacles in your home to promote healing.

What do you do when you return home with a broken heart?

As a physical therapist, interior redesigner and a widow, I have found changes in surroundings to be a valuable prescription in grief recovery. A little of my story follows, but this book is not about me nor my design style. This about what you can do to jumpstart your healing and movement through grief.

Introduction

This book is about how to move forward after your loss. Small changes in your home and surroundings can prove to be big changes in your life and mind.

It was during an in-service presentation to a grief group affiliated with hospice care that something changed in me.

The first time I had been in the same room was four years earlier after having lost my husband to lymphoma. At that time I was 49 years old, my daughters had both just graduated from college, and the dog had died. I was turning 50, but that was the least of my worries.

My husband and I had moved 12 times, built 10 homes, and had a repertoire of medical protocols even more numerous. Why more change?

Sitting in the grief group for the first time with women who adored their husbands and donned lockets with their spouses' photos, I wanted to flee. I was angry because I knew I had to change and did not want to do it anymore. A small step forward felt like a lunge over the side of a cliff or a drop into a ravine.

I never went back to the grief sessions until January 2009, when I was asked to speak about interior design changes to freshen the home. My business, called Revival Redesign, helps clients use what they own and love to brighten and enlighten a space.

What spoke to me that night, what refreshed me, was the beautiful internal spirit and soul that each one of the men and women assembled there exuded.

I knew how hard it was to get in a car to come to the session. I knew how hard it was to listen to others speak and tell their story. I knew how much endurance it would take to go home and enter the dark and quiet home and to get into bed. I knew how much honor and love should be bestowed upon them.

I knew that *we* can love and honor them in their grief, but honoring *themselves* through the grief process seemed to be the hardest of all things to do. I wanted that for them!

So in honor of all of you that trudged through the snow on that January evening and all of your silent internal changes, this book is for YOU!

Within the loss of a loved one you have lost more than him or her, you have lost a part of yourself.

Loss need not be partnered with grief, but grief is most often partnered with some kind of loss. In my dialogue grief is interlaced with loss.

In *Room for Change,* some simple and small changes will help lighten your heaviness in grief and give you a different perspective on your home as

In honoring yourself, you honor others.

a haven. These changes can move you forward during this daunting journey.

There are also suggestions for you to offer to those close to you to help you. These ideas are a jumping off place for what outreach may truly give: some respite and care.

Finally, there are resources to help you in your forward motion.

Make room for that love and grace that you so rightly deserve.

Blessings,

Susan

CHAPTER 1

Living After Loss

As you can imagine and as you probably have already experienced, grief presents itself in many different boxes and many different wrappings. There are a normal range of feelings associated with grief, including loss, isolation, instability, anger, and at times immobility.

Grief may be the springboard to enhance the life experiences you are already experiencing. Grief may bring a reevaluation of your future hopes and dreams. Grief may keep you stuck in what was and what is.

How you challenge yourself in and through grief is a unique opportunity for you to be creative, patient, and supportive of you. It may even be the first time in your life when you take the time to ask, "What is it that I want for and in my life?"

It might be harder than you think to find an answer, especially if you have been a caretaker of others for most of your life.

One of the first steps in dealing with grief is to address your home environment. Creating simple changes in your living space can help you heal and grow. I will suggest design ideas in the effort to engage you in the process of the changes that make you feel good, or at least better, from day to day.

Losses can lead to grief, be it the loss of a job, the loss of a person or partnership, the loss of a life purpose, the loss of youth or health, or the loss of dreams. Attachment to these have made you the person you are. Now is the time within this loss to determine whether the attachment facilitates your growth and transition through grief or hinders it.

Attachment can be emotionally great for you or can hinder you in your healing journey. The choice of attaching to something is ultimately yours. You can take those ideas or items and find ones that are supportive.

Items and ideas can be released and repurposed. Now is the perfect time re-evaluate how these fit into your new life.

EXPANDING SPACE

Michael's wife was on hospice and instead of leaving him innumerable decisions to be made after her passing, she presented him with a gift prior to her passing. She made a list of to whom her possessions would go. China was assigned to one son, kitchen appliances to a daughter, clothing to the church outreach center, and jewelry assigned to others. What did this do? It created a different kind of space for Michael. A space of free time to do what he felt he wanted to do instead of what he had to do. He helped friends and neighbors build decks and did home improvement activities. He did not have to second-guess where unused items would be going. He still had a hard time navigating the kitchen without her, but he used the sunroom on the back of the house for his computer and computer gaming. As he entered through the back of the house, the room he had reconfigured for himself was there. Something old and something new were merged. He enjoyed his solitude while playing the games and had the time to help others on their building projects.

One does not always get the chance to say goodbye and make our requests known, but it is a way to ease the decision making of the caregiver or executor of the will if some decisions can be made ahead of time. It also provides boundaries in discussions of whom should get what and can alleviate potential ill feelings in one's grief. Consider the joy of the woman on hospice in knowing that she has cleared the air on her requests ahead of time and new decisions and directions will be less numerous for others as time progresses. Spreading joy and love throughout the death and dying process is possible. Gratitude and love can always be expressed.

One Step at a Time Through Grief

Often in daily life we tend to get ahead of ourselves with the "to do," "should," or "what if" lists that may accompany our decisions. In and through grief, these lists often magnify and may appear never to shrink. Remember your uniqueness, your innate creativity, and your ultimate need to traverse this new uncharted time the way it feels best for you.

Change in grief may be the last thing you want to do. Perhaps you did not want it and you may not have asked for it, but it is here. Your home with all its memories, its textures, and its aromas may seem like the only essence you have left of your loved one. Navigating through your home may feel daunting.

By moving items and ideas out of your life, you are moving energy forward to reconnect with who you are now and what you need or want to be with the new changes facing you.

Grief can be an avenue for small changes that can support you where you are right now. These small changes can move you forward, providing growth for you in simple and practical ways.

I see grace and comfort in small things.

Finding Your New Life in Your Old Space

In grief, some days taking a shower and getting dressed may be all you can accomplish. Answering the phone may feel burdensome.

The following query can be used to jump-start your thinking process about what to hold onto in your new life and what to release. In grief, your responses may change from day to day. Address the following questions if the mood strikes you. They are a simple tool to redesign your outlook on your home and life.

1. What is the hardest part of being in the house since the loss?

2. What brings you comfort in your home these days?

3. What room or rooms do you never use?

4. Where do you spend most of your time when you are at home?

5. Is this place where you tend to settle in a new place created since your loss, or has this spot always been there and brought you pleasure? If the latter, why do you go there?

6. When you enter your home, through which door do you enter? What is the first thing you see?

7. What activities do you perform or participate in at home?

8. What activities do you participate in outside of the home?

9. Have you purchased anything new for the home since the loss? Have you purchased anything new for yourself?

10. Have you given anything away since your loss? What have you considered giving away?

11. What brings you the greatest pleasure in your home these days? Rate the pleasure on the scale of 1 to 10.

12. Do people compliment you on your home and like to have it as a gathering spot? Or do you prefer your solitude?

13. Are there any pieces of furniture that are uncomfortable for you to sit in?

14. Are there any areas of your home that are cluttered, though not necessarily messy? How does that area make you feel? Do you even care about it?

15. If you could change one thing about your home, what would it be? (Forget about limits of money, time, or energy.)

16. Think of a home that you like to be in that perhaps belongs to a friend or a relative. What do you like

about it? What is the feeling that it brings to you? Can you identify it?

What supports you? What simple things can you do in your home to promote movement and healing?

Your journey through grief has started, and you can create the motion through it in small and practical ways. Let's get started!

CHAPTER 2

Making Changes in Your Home

You may have already answered some of the home inquiry questions and have gathered an interest in how to help change items and your perspective in your home. If you skipped the questions, that is fine too. This chapter will give you a jump-start on assessing what you can create for yourself with what you already have in your home and what you know and desire intuitively.

Often people will look to interior designers for the designer's style because they are afraid that what they like is "not enough" or afraid that they do not know what goes together. This chapter is about what you like and what you want to pull together. It is certainly helpful to look at magazines, shows on HGTV (my favorite), or furniture show rooms, but you can, with a gentle prodding, create a space that supports you and welcomes your individuality.

These ideas may help you create some ideas of your own. It is not necessary to tackle every room of your home, nor is it necessary to change something at a certain time during grief. Simply scanning your home for what your daily activities entail and then creating space for these activities is the premise of such overview.

The following subchapters will provide some simple ideas to keep your creative juices flowing and provide practical ways to tweak your home. This will keep you moving forward on this sometimes daunting, sometimes exhilarating journey.

We will start at the front door and weave our way around the most common rooms in the home and then exit through the back door. If you live in an apartment or in a single room, do not worry. The suggestions can still be applied to such a living space.

Our homes provide us with a space to eat, sleep, read, converse, work, create, rest, and nurture ourselves both

Your front door speaks.

physically and mentally. This is what *Room for Change* is about: What supports you! Let's begin.

Your Grand Entrance Through Grief

In grief, some people go into hiding and avoid social contact, while others have family and friends through their threshold constantly. Sprucing up the front door can say "Yes world, come on in," or it can say "I'm needing private time now."

Your grand entrance into your home may be the front door, may be the side garage door, or may be the hallway from the main foyer. In all circumstances, your entry into it sets the stage for you and tells others who may visit. This is the spot where your individual creativity and special uniqueness may abound.

What small changes can you make to your front door to bring pleasure to you and give a hint to others of what you love?

- Hang and herald a statement. This can be as simple as a welcome sign or a plaque with your name or nickname on it. It may be a wreath adorned with flowers or birds, expressing your love of nature. Two years

ago a mother bird found my wreath on the front
door and made her nest. She also made a mess, but
the cleanup was well worth it! If you do woodworking or have fabric art skills, perhaps a piece of your
artwork may be hung upon the door or adjacent to
it. These items are easily changed from season to season and can cost very little.

- Light the way. In the evening it is comforting to know
  upon your arrival home that a light
  is already on outside and inside
  your entrance. A motion sensor
  exterior light can provide exterior
  light as well as safety. A small lamp
  in your entry on a timer can bring a
  welcoming evening warmth upon
  your arrival. Exterior lights that
  flush the yard with ambient light are comforting as
  well. Inexpensive solar light styles abound and often
  require no wiring to cast that evening glow outside
  your door or pathway.

  I gain confidence each day by simply moving one more step.

- Make it noteworthy. There may be unexpected deliv-
  eries or visitors to your doorstep. Friends may send
  flowers or want to leave you a meal. Others may want

to see you and know how they can help. You may
be away or perhaps unable to talk at that moment.
Leaving a notepad and pencil hidden by the door can
facilitate logistics for you and others. It also provides
another welcome form of communication other than
phone or e-mail.

Create your grand entrance with pride. Show them
"your stuff." Enjoy!

Fire Up the Kitchen

The old saying that the kitchen is the heart of the home
still holds fast. The kitchen is a preparation area for
building the nutrition for your body and a place that
brings people together for both planned and unexpected visits. You may find yourself using the kitchen in
a different manner during grief or maybe simply viewing
the heart of the home in a different light.

Refreshing the kitchen to uphold you may take
on different directions, but look how this room can
support you. What changes could be mustered to
strengthen you?

If you have appliances on your countertops that you do not use on a daily basis, this may be the time to find another home for them or put away out of sight. Creating more counter space can open up your mind, a simple way to declutter. Consider giving extra appliances to family members who may use them more frequently or maybe donate them to a local high school home economics class. Many thrift shops connected to churches or community organizations will welcome them as well.

Updating your kitchen can include a new paint color (the least expensive and often easiest way to freshen a space), changing out old fluorescent lighting fixtures to recessed lighting, or adding pendant lighting for task work. There are lighting kits on the market that allow one to transform a recessed light to pendant lighting. As suggested in the upcoming section on lighting, light carries with it a subtle healing power and helps you use areas in multiple ways with ease.

Use plants and herbs and colorful fruits and vegetables in your kitchen to brighten your space. It can be nurturing for you to nurture your plants. If your thumb is not green, silk plants can provide a softness and color to the sharp and hard surfaces that often accompany many kitchen surfaces.

Beside the sink, add a new fragrant soap or beautiful item that makes you smile. I added a piece of pottery that could get wet in my sink. It is a soapstone carved face from Africa. When I drain the sink, his face is looking at me. (I know it sounds crazy. What is more fun is when friends ask, "What is in your sink?!!") Remember what brought you joy as a child. Bringing some unexpected pleasures back into your life is a possibility. When you are not using something, pass it on. You do not have to be the caretaker of all the items under your roof. Pass them on!

Try setting up a tray on your counter to be ready to transport your meals to another space, or even just to the kitchen table. My favorite trays are translucent, made of a Lucite material. I can then place a colorful plate of my choosing on it as my mood suggests or add a pleasing placemat.

The tray can hold my condiments, my drink, and even a magazine or remote control. The tray is also a good place during the day to place mail or to-do lists. Having a regular staging place helps me focus and keeps me from retracing my steps throughout the day. Often in grief our minds get cast from here to there and back again. A central place of operation, like the kitchen, with good lighting, plants, open counter space, and a system can be a great heart of the home and a great way to fire up your day!

Bring into your kitchen the aromas and sights that please you.

Transform Your Dining Space

Your chosen place of dining may have changed during this grief journey, and that is just fine. The importance lies in gathering nutrition wherever you are.

You may find that your formal dining room, if you have one, is seldom used, or maybe even the kitchen table or eating niche is not used frequently.

> **INSPIRING OUTLOOK:**
> 24"–30" is the suggested spacing between wall and dining room chair.

Envision the space you never had but have always wanted, or even envision the space to sprawl things out and keep it that way. Often in grief, we are living a more solitary life and the "have to's" of our partner or friends may not be part of the daily schedule or demands.

Think about making your formal dining into a study or library for yourself or even a sewing room. Often the simple addition of French doors to such a previous formal area can revamp the space and change its function. Pocket doors or translucent sliders are available to hide the "messes" you may wish to leave out.

If you are not using your kitchen or dining room table for eating these days, how can it be used? Do you do crossword puzzles? Think about placing a fresh mug of No. 2 bright yellow pencils on your table. Add a bowl of red and green apples if they are something you might partake of as well. Maybe you are a jigsaw puzzle aficionado, so give yourself permission to leave the puzzle out and tackle it when the mood strikes. Maybe you love scrapbooking, and the dining room table that never gets used can be laden with boxes of your materials and stacked with photos in a simple wicker basket. Think about making the area fun and functional as well. Did you always want a pool table or air hockey table for when your family came over? Not using the formal dining room? Change it into a billiards room! Why wait? Make your home your haven.

TRADING PASSIONS

Rhonda's husband died. He had been an avid collector of miniature trains, which circled his home office. She was reluctant to change the room but found no pleasure being in the room. I suggested she inquire of family members whether any had interest in a train set and that the others be boxed away or auctioned off for money for herself or her grandchildren. She then told me she did not want an office. What did she like to do? She loved scrapbooking. Together we made subtle changes. The present shelves that had been the train track in the office allowed a place for scrapbooking materials to be stored. The desk now contained other practical supplies for her project, and it was repositioned so she could view the outdoors. She was amazed and excited to have a place for her to do an activity that brought her pleasure. With her scrapbooking, she could use her love to create memory books for her family in a setting she recreated for herself.

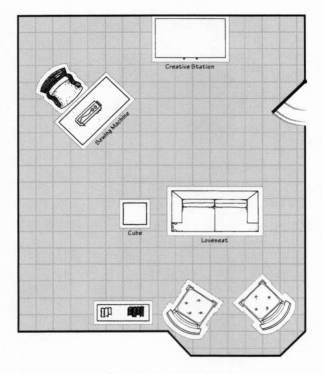

Three activity centers

Repurposing a room is possible. Make it your own.

This room was divided into several activity centers. One is for sewing and crafts. One is for reading and the other for group conversations. Decide how you want to use your space and invite activity.

Creating Your Nest

As we find ourselves walking through grief, we may also find ourselves sitting still in grief. The living room that might have held the family activities of times past may seem like an underused and oversized cavern of memories. Many newer homes have replaced the conventional living room with the "great room," making the delegated space for a smaller family feel challenging.

Your living room or your nesting spot may be ready for some transition. Some suggestions follow.

> **INSPIRING OUTLOOK:**
> 18" is the suggested spacing between a sofa and coffee table.

- Capture the view. Reposition the sofa to catch a better view of the outside or move a rocking chair next to a window with a small reading table beside it. Nothing but nature provides unsolicited entertainment.

- Take a leap. Move the sofa away from the wall. It will not necessarily make the room look smaller and may provide a coziness that is most welcome. Covering the sofa with a slipcover in a soft chenille or ultrasuede fabric may be comforting in your reclining times of repose.

- Punch it up. This is the time when some vibrant or new color pillows can dazzle you with little expense. You may want to add a burst of color with a small area rug to anchor your sitting area, thereby making it feel more intimate.

- Light it up. Remember that besides opening the drapes for natural light, up-lights behind plants, floor or table lamps, and full-spectrum lighting to rid the "blues" are all comforting.

- Swap meet. Swap out a sofa for two oversized chairs. The chairs need not match; they only need to have a similar proportion to each other. You can be cradled in such a chair, and when company visits the conversation may be more comfortable than on a large, solo piece of furniture. If the loved one you lost has a favorite chair sitting vacant, sliding it into another room may be helpful in your transition through grief. If it fits you and its presence harbors no terrible memories, let it be. Give yourself permission to change things and change them back again. Nothing is static.

- Nesting notes. If you have a difficult time moving around the house, set up your nesting spot, wherever it might be, with some of the following: phone, notepad and pencil, tissues, and a pleasant scented candle or diffuser with essential oils. If in the past you always burned a vanilla scented candle perhaps a peppermint or citrus would be suggested to assist with concentration. All of the above may assist you, along with some freshly brewed chamomile tea or a warm soup. Taking time to rest is a gift you give yourself.

My daughter reminded me during my time in grief of RINAWOT. "What is that?" I asked. RINAWOT, she told me, stands for Resting Is Not a Waste of Time! Be kind to yourself. Naps are refueling.

INSPIRING OUTLOOK:
Use rugs to anchor seating and
to encourage conversation.

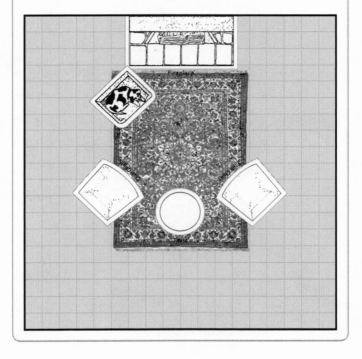

Changing the position of items in your nest can help
you relax and refuel in a time of changes.

Wherever you may land these days, look for a way to maximize your comfort and bring some new insight to all that surrounds you. Make it your way and make it comforting!

INSPIRING OUTLOOK:

Be brave. Step away from the wall with furniture. Placing furniture away from walls can create room for secondary task areas and allow more flow options.

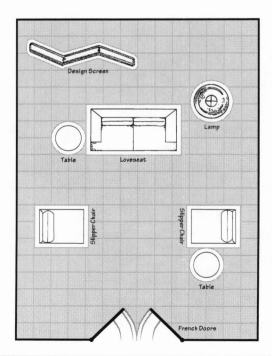

Invite intimacy.

MAKING THE LIVING ROOM LIVE AGAIN

Nancy's husband had received the services of hospice related to his respiratory collapse. She also had to move from her family home into a new community and smaller home to be closer to family for her husband's care.

The hospital bed and his care had occupied the guest room, and the living room had been the place where the other medical equipment was housed. Nancy felt an overwhelming gloom in the rooms. Together we addressed two areas. First, we looked at the living room and its function for her. The sofa was hurting her back, and the chair her husband sat in was uncomfortable. We rearranged the living room, creating a seating vignette with the rocking chair, from another room, that was comfortable for her. We added appropriate lighting for reading next to the chair. The view from the chair also allowed her to see people coming and going outside. We changed the focal point of the room from the sofa to a beautiful well-worn desk that had belonged to her father adorned with tall silk flowers in a crystal vase from her corner display cabinet. A mirror was placed to the right of the door to let her check herself out on coming and going, and a tray to put keys and incoming mail sat there as well.

The room in which the hospice care was given was transformed with a convertible bed/sofa for guests that also fit her small frame for reading. She bought a new tiffany style lamp to pick up the colors of the rug already in the room, and her husband's chair was placed in the corner to give guests a place to read or place their belongings.

Memories were not lost or forgotten in the process. Nancy said, "I cannot forget, but when I come into the house now, I do not see the oxygen tank and cords."

Sleep or Slumber?

While traveling the walk of grief, the days and nights frequently meld into one.

At night it is hard to sleep; during the day it is hard to focus. A good night's sleep is at a premium. Allowing small changes to occur in your bedroom may help you achieve the slumber that is paramount to your health.

Refreshing your physical space can help transition your sleep time to restorative slumber.

The bedroom, which often serves as a full-service care center for many days in the caring of a family member, may linger with memories that keep one from moving forward.

What changes can you make to your bedroom to keep you moving forward?

- Take a look at your bed. Is it possible to place it in a different position within your bedroom? Can you put it on an angle? Can you change out the headboard to another one in your home? Could you imagine downsizing your bed size from a king to a queen? Maybe the mattress is ready for an upgrade. Remember that your mattress is one of those items you use every day. Make certain it gives you the support you need for the rest you need. This may be the perfect time to sleep on something new.

- Buy yourself a new set of sheets. You may want to switch to some flannel sheets to keep you warmer. You may consider a bright pattern or your favorite color on a new set. Try switching out the bedspread

Bedside ingredients for a good night's rest

to a comforter. If you have lost weight and are feeling colder at night, a down comforter that cuddles and cradles you may be in order. A silly stuffed animal or your own pet may be another welcome addition to the bed.

- Set the stage for sleep. A simple vase or glass jar with a single fresh flower and a battery-operated candle next to your bed along with an inspirational book can be helpful to settle in. It is comforting to gaze at something beautiful and awake to the same item in the morning.

- Let the light in. Heavy curtains do not let the light in. Transitioning to sheers might lighten the room. Seeing nature and light is powerful in healing your body and mind. A bird feeder placed outside your window allows you to glimpse the simple pleasure of motion.

- Follow the fragrance. Lavender essential oil in a diffuser, lavender-scented candles, or dried lavender at the bedside can sweetly assist slumber.

- Put your worries down. Place a notepad and pencil at your bedside for those nighttime inspirations or worries and cast them aside while you sleep.

Sweet dreams!

A Closet Full of Memories

One of the most difficult spaces in the home to address after the death of a loved one is the closet.

The clothes, being the closest physically to our loved ones, plus the memories associated with certain clothes, can create an overload on our senses and keep this spot a place most difficult to address. I have found that this space often requires the help of family, including the children and outside assistance, whether it be professionals or volunteer organizations.

If you are "stuck" or lost on what to do with the closet, some suggestions follow. Again, as in all grief work, there is no timetable. Change will come, but often change can come sooner if there is physical room to grow. The closet is often one of the first big steps in this change. This is one place where removing an item may feel like we are casting away the memory. It need not be true. Memories will survive and flourish.

Consider the following: If you are not going to be using it, make it purposeful and donate it to someone who can use it or to an organization that will. Consider this recycling for the planet and a gift to others. Many churches or social organizations will gladly pick up clothes. After the death of my husband, a local missionary and his wife came and collected my late husband's clothes and they were sent to Africa. My daughters and I discussed a few items to keep and put them into a large clear storage bin to review later in time. When we asked if family members wanted the items, some were afraid to say no. Remember that their lack of desire to have items owned by the deceased does not necessarily mean they do not care to carry on the memory. Some people are more visual or tactile than others, and some people prefer to carry their memories without many objects near to them.

Several suggestions for using the clothing that may be in the closet or dresser drawers follow. Make a quilt out of different pieces of clothing to give to needy children or donate to an organization. One person I knew opened up the old ties and sewed them together to create a table runner. My church has a quilting circle that will gladly accept materials and fabric to repurpose into a quilt or blanket for those in need. Another person took her mother's old costume jewelry from a dresser drawer and glued the random pieces onto Styrofoam balls tethered with ribbon. These created Christmas ornaments for her family members. Would you consider gluing such items onto a box or even a glass vase to hold flowers and catch the dancing light? This may be an opportunity to enlist the services of a friend that sews to create something for you.

This is also a time when the services of a professional organizer or interior redesigner may be of benefit. Professional organizers can work with you to evaluate what you have, what you need, and what can be donated or sold. It is a way to incorporate a more neutral decision maker into the path of change. Many redesigners also do "clutter control" and have an eye for repurposing items. They know how to transform any existing space into a more efficient, practical, or beautiful setting for you without purchasing items. An example of this may be using a closet that is not holding clothes anymore as a study or office area. Closet doors may be removed, and the cubicle now created can house a desk or shelves to provide that niche to work, write, or use a computer. A mirror placed inside the closet can open up the room, thereby bringing in more light and creating a more spacious feeling. I transformed a small walk-in closet into my office by placing a free-floating desktop in it. When my "workday" is finished, I simply close the door. The room is painted a bright tropical turquoise, while everything else in the house remains a cool neutral. It provides a fun working space that is unique to me.

Closets that are cleaned out can also house a dresser, thereby freeing floor space in the room. The newly discovered space could perhaps accommodate a chair to create a reading nook, or another place to call your own. Closets are a great place to experiment with fragrances you might enjoy within their confined space. Diffusers or air fresheners are economical. Find one that is pleasant to you. Using extra closet shelves to house a collection or even a few photos is also a possibility. I always find a place to prop a child-hood doll of mine. The whimsy of spotting her from time to time helps keep me lightened up!

Remember that there are people and organizations willing to help you move forward when you are ready.

I am important, loving, and loved in my solitude and self reflection.

Enlist whatever support you need. Others can benefit from what you can offer to donate or sell.

Reflections on the Bathroom Mirror

Each day we rise, often before the sun itself, and the first place we frequent is the bathroom. It is surely one of the most personal and private spaces in our home. We look at ourselves in the mirror, reflecting upon our physical image as well as our thoughts for the upcoming day. If we have cared for our loved one at home, the bathroom may house remnants of caretaking along with many personal items of our loved one or remind us of the loss.

What changes might one make to brighten this room?

- Remove the toiletries, medical supplies, and/or assistive devices of your loved one.

- Donate any unused medication to an organization such as "Doctors Without Borders" or a local hospice organization. Pharmacies will readily dispose of medication for you, and it is safer for the environment than putting it down the drain.

- Many churches or charities are grateful for donations of assistive devices and will come to collect them. If it is difficult for you to do, ask a friend. Friends are always looking for a "job" that is truly needed and appreciated.

- Bandages, IV supplies, etc., placed into ziplock bags can also be dropped off to nursing homes or community action organizations. It can be comforting to know someone else is going to benefit from your donation.

- Place a small flower or plant by your sink and mirror. Seeing its growth and natural beauty is uplifting as you pass by or brush your teeth.

- Add a new and comforting fragrance to your bathroom to pleasantly greet you.

- A silly picture of you and your loved one taped to the mirror may help you find a smile and bring gratitude for all that was and is!

- A new set of towels in your favorite color is a great morning greeting, or you may want to splurge on a new soft, luxurious towel. It need to be only one.

- Last but not least, clean the mirror to see the beauty in you!

Savoring Your Exit

Just as with a great novel or intriguing play, the last words written or scene last viewed get burned into our senses.

As you exit your home, often not through the front door but back or side door, what do you see, hear, or feel?

Is the garbage can encroaching on your exit? Or are you stepping over items to be taken to the neighborhood shelter? Are your boots and mismatched gardening gloves on the nearest surface, surrounded by recycling that needs to be addressed?

By creating a smooth, clean, and calming exit from your home to the outside world, you can carry a last note of clarity with you during the day. Most of us will have some of the items mentioned above surrounding us, but perhaps an area for staging them could be created. It may be labeled baskets that creates such a system. It may be plastic bins or a simple metal shelving unit, with a different shelf delegated to different tasks, that works for you.

Just as your front door speaks of you, so can your back door. Neatness is not always a virtue, but how you enter and leave your home can quietly reflect how you may view the day.

Your grand finale, your exit door, need not always command a standing ovation, but you deserve a sweet ending to carry with you. Ask your cast (your family) or your understudies (your friends) to help you. You can then all applaud the performance.

Nurturing Nature

Much is being said these days about creating a haven within your home. Much can also be said about extending that haven outside.

You may already have a patio or screened porch to enjoy the morning breeze and the songs of the awakening birds. If you do, do you use it? A comfortable chair, a solar lamp, or an indoor-outdoor rug may be all that are needed to add a functional outdoor space to your home.

Portable fireplaces or pits can bring you and your company outside on a cool evening to enjoy the stars and evening air. Any small change in setting in grief can

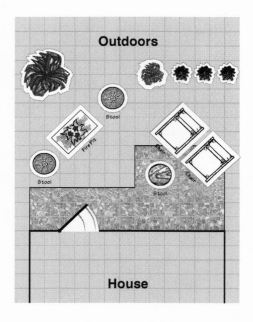

*Expand your experiences and
senses with the outdoors.*

stimulate your senses and may provide unexpected sur-
prises to an old routine.

The bounty of a garden, however small, can also
extend your home. My last garden was simply a long
rectangular window box that contained fresh herbs.
The herbs hung from my privacy fence by my grill. As

I grilled, I would pluck my favorite to flavor the food and aroma that evening. The time investment was not huge, and seeing the herbs grow was something I joyfully anticipated.

If gardening is not your forté, perhaps assembling a birdbath or bird feeder close to a place that you sit outside may hit the mark. Even the pesky squirrels can bring some levity to a gloomy day with their resourceful antics.

The addition of a hammock or porch swing is also a simple way to create an outdoor space that invites a book, a cup of coffee, a magazine, or even a nap. Rest and renewal is very important during the grieving process. A soothing and tranquil space incorporating the outside and nature does double duty in assisting the healing process.

Outdoor spaces can be created

- by placing potted plants around a designed area that you like to be within;

- by placing an indoor-outdoor rug on a patio or even a grassy area (one that can be hosed down to clean);

- by putting up a garden umbrella or canopy with table and chairs;

- by placing inexpensive bamboo screening in a desired area to create privacy as well as a windscreen;

- by hanging weather-resistant roman shades along side of a porch so as to create more privacy and a haven for yourself; and

- by using a trellis alongside porches or deck.

The above suggestions are simple ways to extend your inside out or your outside in. If you have an outdoor space, you may want to reinvent it for a time. What's the worse that could happen? You can put it back! Allow for experimentation during your grief process, in your setting and in your activities. It can open unexpected pleasures for you and others.

CHAPTER 3

Uplifting Your Atmosphere

One definition for the word *atmosphere* is "the dominant mood or emotional tone of a work of art." In and during grief is the perfect opportunity to look at your home as your work of art and assess the mood or emotional tone it suggests to you.

The last chapter walked you through your space, looking at some of the foundational rooms or areas of activity. In creating "atmosphere" in your home, you are layering onto your foundation.

This does not suggest you are putting a blanket over memories and covering up the past; rather, this layering can provide subtle ways to uphold you on your journey.

The first subchapter is decluttering. For me, decluttering is one of the hardest tasks to start but the most rewarding to finish. In presenting it first, like assigning your hardest homework first, I hope to open more room for you to envision the home you desire. Color, aromas, sound, plants, and items that can support your meditative senses will follow the decluttering. As with all chapters, these are ideas to help you find more ideas unique to yourself. Let's layer your work of art!

INSPIRING OUTLOOK:
To create interest, think about color, texture and pattern, and scale.

Controlling Clutter, Opening Opportunities

My procrastination in writing about clutter held me captive for days. As I reflected on this procrastination, I considered several things, and the greatest of these is that I have not been an expert in clutter control. My

Clutter keeps you in the past.

downsizing and purging of items in my life have not been easy. I must admit, it is always easier for me to do clutter control for others and with others. With the death of my spouse, my daughters moving away, and my own transition to a smaller abode, I am becoming more confident in my abilities, but even more confident in the profound effects that controlling clutter can create for those in grief.

In grief, decluttering offers room for growth in your physical setting and in your mind. Items attract our attention in ways both great and small. Too much clutter can make it difficult to bring something new into our environment, or even too difficult to find something cherished already existing in it.

In grief, our minds as well as our environments can be cluttered with things, with thoughts, with decisions to make that we may have not been prepared to make. In decluttering or redesigning our physical environment, one's goal is to put back items that support, not hinder. Perhaps the mind-cluttering and activities we perform could also use a bit of redesigning.

Clutter affects different people in different ways.

Clutter can

- keep you in the past;

- confuse you;

- be unhealthy physically and even a fire hazard;

- decrease financial resources available to you: insurance, storage lockers, maintenance, and cleaning;

- keep you ashamed: limiting access to your home by friends and family; and

- keep you fatigued: just thinking about the clutter can "tire" you.

According to Karen Kingston, author of several books dealing with clutter and energy, clutter can be divided into four categories:

- things you do not use or love

- things that are untidy or disorganized

- too many things in too small a space

- anything unfinished

This time of transition in your life is also a great time to reap the benefits of purging or clearing the house of the items above. This is also a task that friends or professionals can assist you with. There is no hurry to do it all at once, but little tasks like cleaning out your "junk" drawer one day will offer you a sense of accomplishment and create some order in your life.

The first thing to do is assess an area to tackle, be it the junk drawer, the front closet, or even your coffee table or bookshelf.

Second is to set up a simple system. Four piles or boxes are a good start. One pile is for donation, recycling, or selling. Selling could be done through a garage sale, Ebay, or Craigslist. This is a prime opportunity to enlist your friends' help. The second pile is for trash. The third pile is to save. The fourth pile can be items that will be going back to the drawer, closet, or shelving. If you do want to save something, label it with a listing of general contents and the date it was packed. My preference is a clear bin that can easily be accessed if I need something. If I do not go and seek something within a year in that bin, chances are that I do not need it. Of course important tax papers or receipts are an exception. If what you want to keep is a keepsake item, keep

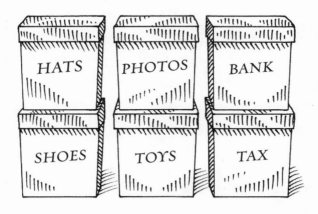

Create a system.

them to a minimum. If the keepsakes are for someone else, maybe you can box them up and give them to them now, freeing up some space for yourself.

To reiterate, clutter tends to keep you in the past, keeps you tired, confuses you, makes you ashamed to have people in your home, keeps things on hold, entails extra time and energy to clean, and is a health and fire hazard.

POSITIVE ATMOSPHERE

Lauren had been helping her son-in-law with her grandchildren. Her daughter had died of breast cancer two years ago. She was looking for some rekindled life in her home since her daughter's passing. With a little assistance, she selected a warm yellow with orange undertones to paint the family room. After the painting, we rearranged the seating to increase some flow so that more people could gather in the room. We also removed many non-functional accessories, which were mostly the accessories that collected dust and nothing more. We regrouped other items into vignettes creating more visual interest. Introducing a silk bamboo plant into a dark corner with some uplighting created a softening to the sharp edge of the large TV, and the ambient lighting was pleasing at night. Both Lauren and her husband enjoy the room now and feel like it is a better gathering place.

Within a few weeks, her husband was in the basement ridding things in his workshop.

Freedom can be found in claiming a space for yourself but also in managing and decluttering a space. One can feel a shift in attitude and sometimes energy when attention is paid to a neglected room. You feel better, and you can welcome others into your space and enjoy it.

There is always the chance that if you stow something away for a while you may not miss it. There is also the opportunity to bring it back out and really enjoy the novelty of this object in your surroundings again. Things are always changing, and providing yourself with a change by de-cluttering creates such space. This space can create wealth and space for others.

Learn to lighten the load. Professional organizers and redesigners are excellent resources to help you jump-start the process. Remember that the task is done in small steps. One drawer at a time or one cupboard at a time is truly enough. What truly supports you? The things? The items? The stuff? Or is it the people around you that support you and what happens within your space? Open it up, lighten it up, and ask for help if needed. You will be surprised what such a space will attract! It will bring a smile, in the least.

May the love I feel in my loss be the gain I carry in my heart.

Consider Color to Enhance Mood

As we tread our way through grief with newly emerging thought patterns, we frequently return to past memories and our heads are focused downward. Our hearts can feel heavy, and our trodden path rather gray and dull. Little seems to spark our interest.

A short time ago I moved to a new town. Everything I viewed was new, but nothing appeared in focus. One new corner looked like the next. Everything seemed gray and nothing sparked my interest, except that I knew this was the place I had landed and it was up to me to find my way. Similar disorientation accompanied me with the death of my husband but on an even larger scale, even

WHAT DO COLORS SAY TO YOU?

"Red gives me energy."

"Peach reminds me
of Grandma."

"Yellow makes me happy."

"Blue calms me."

"Orange makes me feel playful!"

"Green for me
is peaceful."

though I was in the same city I had lived in for years. Little came to life or made sense even in its familiarity.

Color sparked my interest yesterday in this new town as I researched a new exercise routine to get me out of my home on a daily basis. Color also moved me forward. It was a colored hipscarf that sat on a table in a store window in a nondescript shopping mall. The owner sold bellydance items and taught dance lessons in Latin and Middle Eastern dance. I called the owner and was encouraged by her to come try a lesson that evening. That color sparked my interest and moved me forward, making a positive change happen to me in a nondescript, colorless day. It happened to be the first day the owner had placed the glitzy accessories in the window.

I create and color my thoughts with renewed optimism.

Often without thinking, we gravitate towards certain colors, whether it be in the clothing we wear, the wall colors we choose to surround us, or the

INSPIRING OUTLOOK:
When choosing your color palette for your home, think 60%, 30%, 10%. This means your prime choice and a complement with a punch of 10% color!

bedding and towels we use on a daily basis. What colors do you gravitate toward these days? What colors soothe you? What colors make you happy? What colors surround you? You may have found that your favorite colors have changed.

Color therapy, used in complementary and alternative medicine, uses colors for their proposed healing abilities in treating emotional and physical conditions. Its premise is that certain colors cause a set response in an individual. There is, however, a lack of scientific evidence supporting color therapy. Its effectiveness and safety have not been studied completely.

> **INSPIRING OUTLOOK:**
> Select a favorite painting, fabric or magazine photo to jump-start your color selection for creating a new room feel.

Color may not help us heal, but it could help bring of spark of light into a day that feels dreary.

In grief one can feel lifeless, gray, and dormant. Pick your favorite color and splash it somewhere. You can change it, and yourself, each day.

Your Nose Knows

Just as visual memories in grief continue to reflect onto our present daily lives, the sense of smell permeates our home and memories too. We can become so familiar with the aroma of our soap in the shower stall or the fragrance of our loved one's cologne that we no longer smell it. How often have you remembered a smell from your grandmother's house when you were little that wafted past you unexpectedly years later, only to be taken back there within seconds?

Aromas are powerful triggers for memories as well as helpful "friends." Aromatherapy may be a welcome addition to your home during this transition through grief. Aromatherapy may be as simple as burning a scented candle or plugging a diffuser into your electrical wall socket, or even adding cinnamon to the top of your coffee in the morning. It may be opening the windows to the scent of the afternoon breeze and the smell of freshly cut grass or leaving your sheets out drying on a sunny day.

Aromatherapy could include placing cedar chips in your closet of winter clothes or placing a pine-needle sachet in your sweater drawer. All of these may evoke subtle, pleasurable, cognitive changes, unique to each of us. There is no exact formula for what is pleasurable from one person to another.

Some people believe that certain aromas trigger specific physical or mental responses. There are few studies to support such claims. Simply being aware of the aromas around you may inspire new experimentation.

What aromas seem to stimulate your desire to eat? What aromas remind you of a peaceful place where your mind may want to wander? What aromas just smell good to you?

Adding new fragrances to our favorite ones will not help us forget our well-forged memories, but they can help us form new pleasant memories to add to our collection. Memories of our loved ones are packaged with care. Adding additional pleasant aromas is the perfect way to help us move forward through grief. What scents bring you pleasure?

Sound Advice, Icing on the Cake

Without us always noticing it, vibrational sound energy surrounds us as close as the clothes we wear. Experts tell us that sounds resonates in and through your entire body. Sound can sometimes make our skin crawl, like the "nails on the chalkboard" trick or the phone that rings off the wall while the soup is boiling over. Sound can soothe the soul, like the rhythmic lull of the ocean, or comfort us in a warm blanket with the singing of the blues.

We are fortunate to be able to add sounds to our environment, while other sounds we are "stuck" with and hope to mask. I recently moved to a new city. I have never lived where I could hear the train whistle or fire engine siren on my doorstep. I now live a half block from an old brick fire station, and the train tracks are about one mile away. My first thought of the siren and whistle was that they were noise pollution, but now I do not hear them, or when I do I feel a sense of comfort knowing someone is responding and things are moving on.

In grief, we may forget that things are moving forward. Music, the sounds of nature, the tinkling of a wind chime, the drone of the unwatched television, the fish tank bubbling, the swishing and hum of the dishwasher, or the barking of the dog are all sounds that can bring forth a motion in action or motion simply by listening.

Pay attention to what ambient sound is annoying you. Why? What could you use to mask it, or can you remove it? If it is the dishwasher, put it on a timer so it will run at a time when you will be away. If it is a dog barking until

2 a.m. next door, try listening to an ocean music CD, or even using earplugs. Maybe it isn't even the noise, but the lack of it. Listen to music online, in music stores, or on the radio. Find out what genre of music speaks to you or resonates with you these days. You may find that "hits" from your youth give you a lift or maybe classical is calming and moves you through the day.

I found that Middle Eastern and African music was entertaining for me. It made me want to dance, and I couldn't understand the words, so the lyrics did not set my emotions on fire. It was something new that I brought into the house. Now I have explored something new.

Does it mean I carry it with me all the time? Or that I cannot listen to country, new age, or the blues? Never! Music can carry you through tough times and carry you into joyful ones. Music, being so easily portable these days, can be carried from room or room, car to bus, school to grocery store.

Explore what upholds you in whatever you are doing. Be still and let nature speak or create another soothing environment to support you wherever you go.

There are studies available to help direct you to types of music for healing, sleeping, concentration, meditation, or assisting loved ones in dying. You may find these resources helpful. Do not think of it as work to find the "right" music for you. You will know upon hearing if it is right for you at this time. Trust and support yourself with your own sound advice. Sound: It's the icing on the cake, and the best part as far as I am concerned!

Greening Your Space

There is much to be said about "Green Design" in homes and in products for the home. The greening of your space in grief may not even be green, but it can be growth.

Living plants, whether placed outside your window, on your balcony or porch, or even in your bedroom, offer silent benefits to your environment.

- Live plants filter the air.

- Live plants dance in the breeze, creating subtle, soothing rhythms.

- Live plants can provide you nutritional and medicinal benefits.

- Live plants can add beautiful aromas.

- Live plants remind us to nurture ourselves.

- Live plants give us a chance to see growth and something else to nurture.

- Live plants can soften sharp edges of furniture in your home and provide softness to corners of the room.

- Live plants provide shelter from outside heat or a haven for visiting critters.

Some of my favorite plants do double duty. Aloe vera by the sink for cuts and burns. Basil, thyme, and oregano inside or outside for food preparation. Lavender to enjoy the fragrance and encourage the bee population. Roses to partake of their beauty and then to toss into potpourri when dried. Honeysuckle to hold the soil and climb the trellis of an outside wall to provide privacy.

The above are some of my favorites. You will find your own or may already have a garden outside your window or a small windowsill in bloom. Tending to plants, seeing their growth, and sharing their bounty is helpful in moving through grief. It may not be for everyone, but if you have a "green thumb" it might move you forward in your day.

Nurturing yourself and nurturing your plants can go hand and hand—a truly "green" partnership.

Lighting Your Way

Walking a new path may bring with it hesitation and trepidation about the unknown, or excitement and illumination in the possibilities on the horizon. Grief often presents us with both, forming a path that appears to widen and be bright and then narrows and dims with possibilities.

Darkness cannot exist in the presence of light. Physical light can "lighten" our spirits and energy. In grief, there may be even more reasons to consider the sources of light you have surrounding you.

How can you let the light shine in your space to help you move forward?

- Slide aside. Is it possible for you to change out the heavy drapes or curtains on your windows and replace them with sheers or an airy pleated shade that can still provide insulation for your windows?

Would you consider moving the sheers to the side in the morning to let more sunlight shine through and bring more sights of nature in? Simply removing the screens from windows where they are not needed can brighten your room.

- Reflecting beauty. Nothing is easier than a mirror to double the pleasure of something beautiful or bright. Mirrors are inexpensive items that enhance the feeling of space as well as the feeling of lightness. Use mirrors to reflect something beautiful like the outdoors, a chandelier, or your face upon entry into the home. Mirrors are effective in moving energy as well, according to the study of feng shui. Moreover, mirrors just feel good. Just keep them clean!

> **INSPIRING OUTLOOK:**
> A mirror should always reflect something beautiful and/or reflect light to make areas appear larger.

- Shine on through. Glass tabletops on coffee tables or side tables will also reflect interior lighting that you may have close by, or light from outside. Glass also

Reflect light and beauty.

creates a feeling of greater space. Add color to a table-top with serving dishes of crystal or colored glass.

Grab a recycled jar and fill it with mar-bles, stones, or sand. Add a votive candle to it, and another source of brightness can fill your room.

> **INSPIRING OUTLOOK:**
> Create a triangle of lighting in each room and think about how lighting is used for the task at hand.

Using the same idea with coffee beans in the kitchen is practical and easy as well. When the candle warms up, so do the beans, and they waft their aroma!

- Triangle pose. The tripod is a steady and firm foundation. When lighting your room, think of the triangle as well. Try to incorporate at least three sources of light in your room. These sources could be floor lamps, tabletop lamps, overhead light-ing, accent lamps, or low-voltage ambient light-ing. Using a floor lamp with a full spectrum bulb is an extra bonus, as you can get the health benefits of sunshine while indoors. Placing the sources of light into a "triangle" in the room helps eliminate unwanted dark areas.

- Great timing. Consider timers for many of the lights you use regularly. In the winter, it is especially comforting to have the house lit ahead of time. Using energy-saving bulbs is helpful as well.

- Bright ideas. If others are asking how they may help, consider the following. Ask them to wash a few of your windows inside and out, especially the ones you use the most. Suggest to them some of your favorite scented candles, and maybe they could purchase you one or two. The newer soy candles on the market are a healthy alternative to your space. If you like the idea of candles but are concerned about the flame, suggest to them the battery-powered candles that flicker and cast a warm glow. There are others that also have an aroma.

I may feel enveloped in darkness but my light shines in love for others and myself.

Lighting is a simple and economical way to brighten your day. Let that light shine!

Collections and Recollections

Following in the "less is more" mantra, collections and gifts come to mind. My mother always told me "a gift is a gift." That meant when something is given it is up to the receiver to decide what to do with it. How many of you try to find the ugly tablecloth that Aunt Martha gave you last Christmas two days before she arrives for this year's Christmas dinner? You have stored it, and along with it you stored a not-so-great attitude about it. How many of you cannot bear to part with the doll collection that sits in the guest bedroom that nobody uses and collects only dust? Gifts are gifts! Collections are collections!

This transitioning time in grief is a great time to reassess what is really necessary to have around you on a steady basis. Maybe the dolls come out only when your granddaughter comes for summer vacation and are packed away the rest of the year in a plastic bin in the basement. Maybe the tablecloth from Aunt Martha can be donated to another family or used to wrap up gifts for a family you "adopt"

Simply put, simply placed, simply graced: you!

at Christmas. Try to think outside of the box in your use of gifts and collections. If it is not supporting you emotionally, put it into a box and find someone who will cherish the item as much or more than you have.

In Japan, families often have small, narrow closets where they store their collections and artwork. The collection and pieces of art are rotated throughout the seasons. Each "new old' piece is seen as if for the first time on its rotation. Each "new old" piece is seen in a different light and perspective on its rotation. Perhaps you have such a collection to rotate. This can be accomplished with framed photos as well. You can group family photos in one room during the fall and change the grouping out to nature photos of past family vacations in the spring.

> **INSPIRING OUTLOOK:**
> Grouping of items (in three or five) play well off each other. Varying height of items can help interest as well.

EXHIBITING YOUR COLLECTIONS

Phyllis was an artist and writer. Her husband had recently died. She wanted to change something in the bedroom to make it her own. Phyllis loved painting and loved her paintings. She brought in as many as she could and hung them in the bedroom. Hanging a collection of artwork or photos is an ideal way to create a new focal point for the room or heighten the beauty of an existing piece of furniture. Not only did doing this bring her pleasure, it created new ownership in a soothing way. Another layer was added to the room.

Or perhaps a collection, like my white pitchers, can be used in different ways throughout the year. In the summer, my white pitchers catch the light through my window, creating beautiful shadows in the shades of the rainbow. In the winter, they are regrouped together and filled with bright holly and berries. In some of the places I have lived, they have simply rested in a kitchen cupboard waiting to be used for maple syrup for my pancakes or cream for a guest's coffee. Believe it or not, I now use one to scoop my dog's dog food from his bin. Why?

INSPIRING OUTLOOK:
Use items in new ways to repurpose and recycle. A cake stand to hold votive candles as a centerpiece, books stacked on top of each other to make a lamp appear taller, or an old briefcase hung on the wall to collect incoming mail. Use your imagination.

Because I moved into a smaller house, decreased the size of my collection by five, but still had one too many to adorn my new windowsill. Voilà, a new dog food scoop was discovered. I enjoy it daily and hope that Radley, my dog, does too. Repurpose your collections, your gifts. Think outside of the box on their use. Imagine who might offer your "gift" items or collections that do not support you in this new life of yours.

Gifts are gifts. Stuff is stuff. Collections are collections. Let what surrounds you be beautiful and useful.

CHANGE FOCUS

Louise had a difficult time imagining anything in another position in her small home. Functionally, the rooms she had did not offer many opportunities for change. She felt stuck. After we discussed the idea of rotating collections, an "ah-ha moment" occurred.

Above her fireplace hung a dark, dreary painting that her late husband's mother had painted. It was the focal point of the room. She could not envision getting rid of it, yet it brought her no pleasure, and it haunted her knowing it was one of her late husband's favorite items. Artwork is very personal and subjective. This painting pulled both ways on the couple's emotions.

Her idea was to move it to a less-conspicuous place in the room. It may seem like a small change, but it was one that let Louise refocus on something beautiful for herself.

Fireplaces are usually focal points within a room. What adorns yours? It may not be a stagnant piece of art; it could be seasonal items. A cremation urn may sit atop a mantel for some families permanently or for a short time while decisions are being made. If it brings you pleasure to see it, by all means, keep it the focus. Small physical changes can often be grand internal ones.

> **INSPIRING OUTLOOK:**
> Artwork or photos
> can be grouped with
> furniture to add greater
> interest and enhance
> the balance of the room.

In life, memories abound; in grief, even more may surface. You may find as you move from room to room that every surface contains mementos and photos of times past and your loved one. As one moves from room to room, it may be important to have a blank canvas or neutral spots where you are not visually overstimulated. In grief, one may need some short "time-outs" for mini recesses for the mind.

Redefining your collections:

- Less is more. How often does a single rose bring simple delight over the overstuffed bouquet? How often does the simple waft of cinnamon over the heavy spiced meal bring a warm feeling to your senses? It is said that less is more. This can be especially true with photos that settle about the house. Often a single photo is more poignant than half a dozen that clutter a bookshelf. You can always rotate photos from place to place too. Change can help rebirth, forward motion, and progress.

- Mesh memories. Maybe a memory wall with a dozen photos grouped together would have greater impact and visual interest than the same amount strewn about the house. The photos could all have a cohesive theme, with all black-and-white photos, or all black frames, or even all taken during a certain season of the year. Do what feels right for you. This could be a great project for a friend or family member to creatively share their talents with you as well.

Simplifying your surroundings can create space for creative remembrance and open other space for fresh beginnings. These beginnings may sweeten future memories and be added to your wall in time.

Unexpected Support

Some people transition through the changes that grief presents them with daily routine.

The rhythm of the routine helps keep their momentum moving forward in this time of adaptation to many different events and activities in their lives.

Some people take greater moments in this time of grief to be quiet, still, and reflective. They may find personal introspection the insight they need to move forward.

CREATING CENTERS

Laura had a room where she did her daily devotions and reading, a place where her weekly ironing lay, and a closetfull of her deceased daughter's clothing. Together we grouped the books and placed the two bookshelves she owned to create a corner reading area. We opened up the other corner, making it uncluttered except for a candle and the books she was currently reading. Her stereo was placed on a shelf above her reading chair in case she desired some ambient music during her devotion or meditation time. The other corner contained a high-top table where her guitar hung on the wall. On top of the bookcase we placed a grouping of three family photos. Laura and friends of her daughter selected what few clothes of her daughter to keep to decrease the amount of storage needed in the closet. The ironing was placed in a small woven basket behind the door with the iron in the adjacent closet. Now the focuses of the room were in three basic corners: a place to meditate, a place to play music, and a place to read, and she could feel herself settling into any one of them. Creating a task function for parts of your room can be liberating.

In our individual manners of traversing this new road, all ways and rhythms are good, fine, and timely.

In our home environment, simple additions to rooms or windows can assist participating in the rhythm of life, either passively, actively, or both.

- Get closer to nature. Place a comfortable chair next to the window and watch the birds' flight to an outside bird feeder or birdbath. Their sweeping flights and effortless dance can be soothing.

- Let the windows sparkle. A dangling crystal, separating morning sun into rainbows, is an easy way to cast color and movement on your walls. Other sun catchers or an object of inspiration are also beautiful and require no maintenance!

- Wind at work. I have placed a group of butterflies dangling on a fishing line in front of my window and above the heating or cooling duct. When the air starts to move, so do they, in small rhythmic patterns of their own. When the windows are open, they twist and turn to nature's own pattern.

- Water within. Fish tanks or water fountains in the home are ways to bring movement and a rhythmic sense to the moment. Fish have been considered lucky to many cultures and their movement meditative. They can require little care and bring a feeling of contentment and peace to those watching. The water fountain, placed either inside or outside the home, creates a soothing sound without a continual drone. Each splish and splash is unique unto the other.

- Warm the hearth and heart. A fire, whether "faux" or wood burning, can be mesmerizing and soothing as well. There are some very inexpensive freestanding fireplaces or wood stoves that provide the aesthetics of a real fire and also cast heat to the room on demand. The flames, with their unique patterns and lightness, can also quiet our thoughts for a few seconds or minutes, bringing comfort visually or physically.

- Your soothing touch. You may have other ways to bring meditative motion into your home or outside of it. It may be seasonal or may be daily. My hammock in the backyard, which may cradle me for only minutes on an occasional afternoon, is meditative in its movement and requires nothing of me to rest. What is yours?

REDESIGNING AFTER LOSS OF CHILD

I worked with the Jim and Eileen Healy to bring joy to the interior of their home. I will let them tell you about their experience in their own words.

I felt lighter and clearer after we worked on the redesign of our rooms. The clutter left and brightness came into focus. I believe that even though it was cold and winter-ish, the color and openness in the family room seemed to warm me. Spring was springing, and new growth came into play. I felt more organized and intact, and not closed in.

I can't thank you enough for all you did for me and us. You are so talented in so many ways, that it knocks my socks off, and now that's why I am wearing sandals!

Enjoy all that you do, and know my thoughts are with you each day.

Love and smiles,

Eileen

Susan, you know males and feelings. I have enjoyed the change(s) and the simplicity of all the changes. I've always been a proponent of the "less is more" theory. You and Eileen did certainly brighten up our home, and I thank you for helping Eileen with those changes. You probably noticed that when you guys were working I stayed my distance. I was interested but didn't want to get in the way of progress.

Cute story: my son, Dennis, stopped over the other day for the first time in awhile and sat down and looked around. He then said, "Hey, you painted... it looks good. You didn't pick out that color, did you?" See? Everyone picks on me in this family...

The whole concept of redesign is a good one. Once you see the positive effects, you'll be hooked.

All the best,

Jim

CHAPTER 4

Room for Change in Your Surroundings

You have physically or mentally walked the rooms of your home. You have layered the atmosphere to support yourself in grief, and now is the time to address the other surroundings you may find yourself exploring. You may explore some of the same locations as you did before your loss, or maybe this is the time for something fresh. It may be scary, but it also may create some new open doors to pass through. As I tried new surroundings and activities, like library discussions, dance lessons, or even eating alone in a restaurant for the first time, the challenge was to keep things in proper focus.

Just because I tried it once did not mean I had to try it again. Just because I cried the first time I participated in something new did not mean the next time I would. Just because I was solo on this excursion did not mean the next time I would be.

The feeling of the fog of grief lifting, during one of my outside adventures, occurred six months after my husband's death. I was taking a tribal belly-dance class at the local children's world museum. I had never taken such a class but went to try one session. Someone asked why I had come. I responded flatly that I had recently been widowed and wanted to try something that had no connection to my previous years. Another woman overheard the conversation and said that she too was widowed and had started dancing six months after her husband died. She invited me for a quick bite to eat after class at a local restaurant. It was the turning point that opened a previously unopened door. The activity, the perspective, and the friendship were all new and encouraging.

I have the courage to care for myself as well as I care for my loved ones.

The following subchapters may offer insights into supporting yourself in surroundings less familiar than your home as you take your "debut show" on the road. You may find that your "home away from home" is now someone else's home, or it may be your car as you travel to be with a friend. Your home away from home may be the local park or the elementary school as you read to the kindergarten class. My floating homes happened to include the local soup kitchen and the literacy organization. Through that front door came a wonderful young woman from Thailand who became my student and also my friend. She learned English from me, and I learned to love her and her courageous nature, inspired by her exploration of uncharted territory.

As your surroundings change, carry with you the touches of "home" that support you today. You have certainly supported your loved one on their journey down the road; now is the time to support yourself as you travel forward. You have extended your compassion to others, so remember to be compassionate with yourself! A diamond in the rough is still a diamond. Remember that you have a sparkle to give to yourself and others; it may just be the next step you take that reflects that light. Chisel away. You can do it!

In Attitude and Stature

Previous chapters of *Room for Change* have addressed redesigning areas of your home and thereby creating room to change your outlook or perspective. It has also been suggested that simply moving in a different daily pattern can create a more optimistic outlook or help with your grief, if only for a fleeting time.

I am worthy of happiness and joy and expect to find it.

What has not been addressed is how you *feel* in such a space or in other physical settings that you may venture to, like a family gathering, church, a restaurant, or your office. In grief, we often do not know from minute to minute how we will feel, but how we inwardly feel about ourselves can give a positive spin on what occurs outwardly.

You have rearranged your furnishings, your accents, and your lighting. How can you relate that to YOU?

- Your furnishings. Imagine your clothes. Are they outdated? Do they speak to an older vision of you? Are they threadbare or piled in spots? Have you lost or gained weight in your grief process and nothing

Buy something new for you.

seems to fit? If yes, an opportunity awaits. Get back to basics with some simple, classic, or fun clothes. Buy a new pair of slacks that actually fit and can be a standard from which you start a fresh wardrobe. Purchase a blazer or jacket of a texture you love and throw it over a basic skirt or pant. Buy new underwear! If you look good, you will feel good! During my high school years, on test days I tried to wear something new; a vest, a sweater, a necklace. Did it make me feel fresh and new? It did. Did it make my testing skills better? I don't know, but I do know that attitude helps. Confidence to get through trials can increase along with it.

- Your accents. If you have a few basic clothes, think about a bright new purse or shoes to liven your step. Accessories are like paint color on walls in your room. They can be the least expensive way to change and can frame the attitude of what they adorn. Bring some life or sparkle with beads, which reflect light. For men, maybe a new wallet or pair of socks or sneakers can start the process of stepping out into your newly formed world with more confidence and comfort. A new haircut or hairstyle can enhance your stride as well. Maybe change your hair color. If you've never done it before, maybe now is the time. The worse thing that could happen is that you have to change it back again!

- Your lighting. Your smile, your posture, your walk. That reminds me of "mother talk," but body language can work both ways. When you smile, self-healing body chemicals ooze into your bloodstream. These are the good-feeling ones. It can be as simple as a small smile as you observe a child at the bus stop or smiling at a stranger going the opposite way down the aisle in a grocery store.

- Standing tall engages core muscles, which allows greater circulation to major organs and just plain feels better on all your joints than slouching. Your mind during grief could be fighting many battles, and your body often goes along for the ride. Support your body with good posture, moderate exercise, and balanced nutrition. Enlistment of a friend for the above is helpful too. We all need a coach from time to time!

- Give yourself permission to make small changes in redesigning you. Just like changes in your home, small changes in yourself can open other doors and possibilities for positive change in your life. Grief may not feel good, but being good to yourself is a great investment. Treat yourself as you would your best friend: with TLC and love. You deserve it.

Nourishment: Body, Mind, and Spirit

Take a look at the supply of food in your cupboards. Are there items that are outdated, stale, or not used? Can some items be donated to the local food pantry or programs providing meals for others?

Laden your pantry with simple preparation items and nutritious foods that you enjoy. The freezer is also a stashing area to be addressed. You may find welcome or unwelcome guests there!

Nurturing yourself with good food that supports you is important at all times, but especially during grief with the potential stressors of change.

Daily nourishment includes:

- Savor the start. Start your day by honoring the progress you are making. Ideas might include a new mug filled with your favorite drink, the lighting of a new candle as you prepare breakfast, or a fresh quote from an inspiring book. Rewarding yourself for your achievements with gratitude can be a great morning platform.

- Support yourself. With change arises opportunities to create new patterns to support yourself. It could be having dinner in a newly created space or simply adding a new routine. If you find that the television is your dinner partner, go with that. Set yourself a portable tray in the kitchen that can hold a plate, cup, and condiments. Place a colorful washable place mat underneath it for quick clean ups and to prevent sliding. Consider buying yourself a new place setting to bring some newness to the dining experience. You can find inexpensive dishes at a dollar store or even T.J. Maxx. The dishes could have the colors you like, a motif or even a hobby etched into the plate's design. Little pleasures like these are not threatening, and if you change your mind later, the investment was not great. Using a nice piece of crystal stemware often reserved for special occasions or a china plate is also pampering. Why wait? Celebrate the progress you have made, as little as it may seem.

- Consider carryout. Getting carryout and going to a local park to eat is another option for your solo dining experiences. You may be solo, but watching nature or a ball game or hearing children play can have a soothing effect and change your perspective, if only for a short period of time. It may be a great spot to share with your dog as well.

- Request the best. When friends ask what they can do for you, maybe this is the time to ask for some mini-meals that will freeze. You will benefit from the support of friends and from sharing food that can nourish you both. Receiving is as important as giving, so look for opportunities to share this time. Maybe your friends could present you with a packet of "coupons" for a selected number of dinners at their home. Often it is easier to decide when you want to go out and when to stay home, and this option can be helpful for both of you.

- Open up to opportunities. The first time my mother and I went out to dinner after my husband passed away, I cried at the bar as we waited for our table. She asked what was wrong. I spilled forth, "I don't want to be a barfly." She chuckled lovingly and hugged me. Expressing yourself is great. New experiences can be trying but can be rewarding as well. She found "barfly" napkins at a novelty store, and now we have a standing joke. Shortly after my husband died, my father did as well. We laughed with our new roles but could cry with our common stories.

Have basic items stored close to where you will be using them. Your favorite chili recipe may be made in someone else's kitchen as a gift for you. Perhaps extra cookbooks can be given to friends or family members after you have copied your favorites and put them onto your computer for future reference. I have saved several of the recipe cards of my grandmother. They are perfect to pull out at Christmas, and I love to view her handwriting and remember her preparing the ethnic dishes. Pass the tradition on and remember that what you create can become a tradition as well. It is possible to stir things together from a recipe and come up with a new and user-friendly tradition. Traditions are great when they support your journey through grief.

Nourishing your entire body to support your new activities is of utmost importance in moving through grief. If your eating spot has changed, make certain it is comfortable, bright, and colorful in flavor.

Expressing Yourself

The paramount theme in grief is expression. There is no formula for expressing yourself in grief, just as there is no time table or perfect way to traverse the process.

Expression may be simply telling your family members you really want to be alone today or that their advice is welcome but only when you ask for it. Expression may be trying to understand why your late wife's sister demands that the closet be cleaned and finding the words to express your need to put things on hold for a while. Expressing your needs, within your surroundings, is crucial to a flowing grief process. You may have to negotiate with family members on how things are to be handled, but allow your desires to be known.

Expression may take the form of artwork. It may be something you've never done before. Losing oneself in a new activity is really not losing oneself; rather, it is expanding oneself. Perhaps knitting, pottery, woodworking, or jewelry making could stir an emotion. Creating something for someone else and then gifting it is remarkably healing.

Expression through the written word is also helpful. Simply putting an emotion or expression in a journal or on paper can release the words that may be flitting within and bombarding your brain. No need to go back to them; just get them out. Poetry or even a list of feelings you are having can help you see what you are truly feeling and recognize that feelings do and can change.

I never wrote before my husband died. I was afraid to write in a journal because I was fearful of my own feelings being discovered, by myself or someone else. At the suggestion of a counselor, I wrote before I went to bed during the first few months after he died. It helped me get some of the cobwebs out of my head in the often long nights. I have revisited the writings recently, but only to observe the progress I have made in healing. In the grief process, I have learned to express myself through writing. Without the loss, I may have never discovered it.

THE CHANGE IN ME

At the prodding of my meditation teacher who became my mentor and friend, I wrote a small piece about a photo of a horse in skeletal form. I have never written creatively before except for high school projects. I came upon the writing today as writer's block descended upon me (I think it should be called thinker's block instead). I decided to rewrite the horse story, hoping to conjure up other insights that may be dormant, waiting to explode or at least seep forth! This is for Marcie, my teacher.

AUSTIN, THE HORSE STORY

It was a surprise to happen upon Austin. I could not tell if he was ready to be released from where he came or if his emergence from the soil still stunned him. He pranced and danced in the sunshine with no knowledge that I looked on. His transparency was like a dream, yet he was solid and firm, as if nothing could push him over or wear him down. I was afraid to whisper, afraid to let him know of my presence. There remained an innocence in his stance and being.

Gathering the nerve to disturb his dream stance and solitude, I reached into my pocket for the red apple left over from lunch. The wispy threads of the lining of the pocket whirled off of the apple on the wind. Stepping toward his left flank, I lightly tossed the apple and it rolled in a squiggly line, lodging in a worn patch of grass. My silent prayers went out for Austin to discover what and who he was and, if he chose to be among us, to know that we acknowledge him and will care for him.

What did I learn? Perhaps we are not as transparent as we seem to be. Perhaps others try to create our reality, but only we can come to life and participate in it, when we are ready.

So he then donned his finest saddle and nodded his head and asked, "Are you ready to ride?"

I nodded and said it would be my honor. I hadn't thought about it before, but my sign, Sagittarius, is portrayed as half-horse, half-person. In that instant, upon the weathered saddle and his sun-drenched legs, I became one with him. What a moment!

I am strong in my choice to make new decisions and travel unknown places.

Expression may take the form of dancing or singing in the local community choir.

Expression may be creating a community garden. Expression may be talking to strangers in a bereavement group.

Expression is not good or bad. Expression just is. Allow new venues and activities to fill your space and support you on your journey in and through grief. Express your unique and growing self!

On the Road Again

Change your outlook. Change your perspective. Change your location. All three of these can create unbridled opportunities for you.

During my first "solo" Christmas, a friend presented me with an overnight bag decorated with dogs in bright red. Would I have picked that out myself? Probably not. Did I use it? Still do, but now it holds my hip scarves when I travel to dance class. (Did I belly dance before my husband died? Not a chance.)

My friend suggested it as my new overnight bag, and I am suggesting one for you. In addition a list of things to tuck into it is suggested. Let's call it the "Sunrise Satchel." This satchel and spontaneity will keep you afloat. Place it in your car (or closet) and you will always be ready.

Here are some suggested contents for your satchel.

- water bottle and tea bags (You can always get some hot water or put your tea bags in your water bottle and place it in the sun, for sun tea.)

- a journal, magazine, and local map

- a change of clothes, PJ's, and a toothbrush

- a flashlight

- a 20 dollar bill

- a small directory of important phone numbers

- a small appointment book

- a small bag of nuts and/or dried fruit

This satchel is not only for overnights. This bag helps when you may just need a respite. It is also great

Sunrise satchel

for any road emergency or an impromptu afternoon in the park. With the basics wrapped in your satchel, you are on the road again.

Go pick out that satchel. Get one that is out of the ordinary and extraordinary, just like you! Have fun and safe travels.

Pedal to the Metal

During your time of traversing through grief, you may be going places you previously did not consider. You may be traveling here and there, and your car is your home on the road. Some of you may be using public transportation and not be able to address changes in how you travel, but those with vehicles can.

Your departed partner may have been the primary driver or perhaps his or her vehicle sits in the garage. This is a time to evaluate how your home on the road supports you from place to place.

This could be a time when you donate an extra vehicle in your possession to a relative or to an organization for tax purposes. Maybe you can sell the vehicle to help pay bills or even to provide you an opportunity for a trip you have always wanted to take.

Assess the vehicle you are using and see if it truly fits you and your needs. Is the seat comfortable and can you operate the vehicle with ease?

If your loved one had the perfect truck and you are not a truck person, maybe this is the time to trade in for a mid-size SUV. If you have always wanted a place to transport the dog around, maybe a small wagon is something to think about purchasing. Your dog might be your steady sidekick these days, and considering him or where you may be traveling could be important. Are you putting more miles on the car and not handy at maintenance? Maybe a new vehicle would fit the bill. Most newer vehicles have warranties and roadside assistance programs, which are handy for flat tires or any breakdown while on the road. If you do not have AAA, this may be a gift for yourself or something someone might purchase for you.

If a new vehicle is not on the horizon, how do you "feel" in the present car? Is it cluttered with old receipts and food wrappers? Is the carpet stained and the floor mats ladened with dirt and old maps?

Consider having the car detailed. A good wash and wax and even the addition of your choice of fragrance can lift your spirits. Having trouble concentrating and getting lost in you new life? Maybe a GPS would be a welcome addition to your car. If your spouse always cleaned your vehicle, do not feel you have to do it all or do it the way they did. Allow yourself options for how you are living and traveling in your life as it is now.

Lastly, remember to put your satchel in the car and surround yourself with music, books on tape, or talk radio. Maybe this is the only place where silence is your companion. Do what you want to do. Your home away from home should be just that: a place to support you on the move. Buckle up and enjoy the ride. You never know where this new road will take you. Happy trails!

Supportive Spaces

"Oh, the places you will go," as Dr. Seuss exclaims! With the many new and awakening choices you are making in grief, some are demanded of you and some are chosen by you. One of the choices you have is to discover what kind of environment, besides your home, you choose to surround you.

In your solitude, a local library may be a public space that provides you with movement of people yet not forced interaction. It will have fresh new magazines and publications awaiting your perusal or travelogues or reviews to engage you. Remember that what you do today, you do not have to do tomorrow. Often simply trying something is enough to lead you somewhere else with better or more appropriate footing.

Look at the space you choose to go. If you have enjoyed community theatre in the past, maybe a subscription to the next season is in order. I have frequently bought two tickets and then invited different friends. If I did not feel like going, I gave them away as a treat for someone else.

The classroom, whether it be local school evening sessions or investigative classes at the community college, are possibilities for you. Your mind can be stimulated, and the rhythm of a weekly class gives some semblance of order to your week.

Do not underestimate the power of volunteering when you are in grief. I volunteered at the local soup kitchen and smiled when I thought I could not. There is much to be said about the appreciation of others, on both sides of the counter. I also volunteered with preschoolers during their gym session. How can one not see the grace and love in the little children? One particular 4 year old asked me, "How old will you be on your birthday?" I replied that I am 49. She retorted, "That is not what I asked you." I learned a lesson in listening. She then told me that was a big number and that when my birthday came my head would hit the ceiling! Of course she was referencing the fact that I am already 6 feet and with every birthday children get bigger and taller. Her precious words stuck and the smile did too.

Maybe you like to dance but are reluctant to do so without a partner. Line dancing, ballroom dancing, contra, and square dancing all provide solo opportunities to step out in a safe and encouraging space. If art has been a passion for you and has been laid aside, maybe a pottery or photography course will fit the bill. There are many short-term class schedules in most community arenas.

The quest is to place yourself in spaces that support your authentic self and the opportunity to use your talents or to try new activities. This is a time of self discovery and also a time to test the waters in your own boat. What floats your boat? It may be something different these days. Give it a try. The shoreline is not far away and the breeze is fine! Happy sailing.

CHAPTER 5

Room for Supporting You

No More Casseroles, Please

As you grieve, many friends, relatives, and neighbors want to help but do not know how. Too often the help comes too early the first month when you are not ready to receive or even know what to suggest to them that may truly help you. When you are ready to receive, make those around you aware of your needs.

I am upheld by the love of others.

Support from friends

Below are some suggestions, other than casseroles. If you are that friend, consider asking the griever if your outreach would feel "right" to them. If you are that friend, honor the griever and do ask permission. Asking them empowers them and rewards you in knowing that a need is truly met. Casseroles are still great, but here are other ideas.

- Give your friend a grocery list and have them deliver the items to you.

- If you are not a cook and have kitchen items, swap the items with the friend in exchange for one meal a week for 6 months. Maybe make it a Tuesday tradition for each of you.

- If you have tools or equipment in the garage you are not using, donate the tools to the friend and ask to exchange for "X" numbers of handyman service hours in the next year!

As a friend, consider the following:

- Leave a new magazine or short note on the doorstep for 8 consecutive weeks without speaking. Just ring the doorbell.

- Deliver food in one-serving containers that can be frozen. Light meals, like soup, chili, and pot pies, where multiple ingredients are mingled, are best. This means good taste, good nutrition, and ease of preparation.

- Placing an affirmation into an inexpensive frame or send a new one each week. We all love to get surprise packages.

- Offering to have your lawn service cut their grass or shovel the snow for 3 months.

- Give a flower a week for 52 weeks. Place the flower in recycled jar and leave it on the doorstep. Kindness abounds.

- Give your friend a comfort box to open when they are ready. Place inside: new slippers, Twizzlers, a candle, a book of short stories, an Etch-A-Sketch, a glass ornament for a window, a fuzzy blanket, and a stuffed animal with name tag to fill out for it. Allow fun!

These ideas are stepping stones for your creativity. The only rule is "No Rules Allowed."

May those of you in grief find comfort in the small changes you make in your life. You are a champion and deserve the honor bestowed upon you. Abundant blessings await you!

Final Blessing

Often we are too busy looking ahead to see what is beneath our feet. We trample what is waiting to sprout, whether it is new ideas or relationships or even the chance to feel an emotion that has been dormant and is awaiting its time of renewal.

It is the beginning of spring today, and I am thankful for friends that listen, dogs that bark, tears that cleanse, hands that heal, and words of wisdom that teach. One unknown solitary person answered the phone today and gifted me with inspiration and faith and the excitement of new prospects in my life.

Look down, look up, look around. It is amazing what may sprout in unexpected places.

My blessing to you and all that surrounds you.

Online Resources

Grief Support

- **www.growthhouse.org**—Growth House Inc., a comprehensive collection of reviewed resources for end-of-life care and grief

- **www.beliefnet.com**—Beliefnet, a variety of articles related to faith, spirituality, inspiration, and religion

- **www.livingwithloss.com**—*Living with Loss Magazine*, a magazine dealing with loss issues from death, pet loss, job loss, and relationship changes, offering support and inspirational stories

- **www.griefnet.org**—GriefNet, resources for all kinds of loss

- **www.widowspath.com**—Widowspath, connection for widows with other widows and support resources

- **www.sslf.org**—Soaring Spirits Loss Foundation, resources for widows, networking, and conferences

Home Ideas

- **www.hgtv.com**—Home and Garden Television, site of home and garden ideas, contests, and inspiration

- **www.benjaminmoore.com**—Benjamin Moore and Co., interactive rooms to color yourself and a plethora of ideas on how to use color in your space

- **www.associationofdesigneducation.com**—Association of Design Education, a directory of redesigners and interior designers in your area and class offerings for you

Recycle and Donation Sites

- **www.goodwill.org**—Goodwill Industries International Inc.

- **www.salvationarmy.org** —The Salvation Army

- **www. craigslist.com**—Craigslist

Home Organization

- **www.napo.net**—National Association of Professional Organizers, professional organizers resources and locator

- **www.weredesign.com**—Interior Redesign Industry Specialists

Products

- **www.youngliving.com**—Young Living Oils, therapeutic-grade essential oils

- **www.iamsoulnotes.com**—Soul Notes, affirming jewelry and oils

- **www.movebeyondgrief.com**—Move Beyond Grief, journal and writing ideas

- **www.canvascorp.com**—Canvas Corp LLC, space planning kits and creative home decor

About the Author

Susan is certified in the art of interior redesign and is a trained physical therapist. Susan has experienced her own loss with the passing of her husband in recent years. She now calls on her training and experience to help those in grief and their caretakers understand and visualize how their surroundings can be rearranged to provide comfort and growth during their recovery from grief. Susan works through her company, Revival Redesign, to help people refresh and enlighten their personal space using items they already own and love.

She provides downsizing assistance, color consultations and room makeovers. Susan's training in wellness and ergonomics have given her special and sensitive insights into the needs of people. Her love of nature, form and function are at the heart of her simple, practical and economical style of redesign.

Made in the USA
Lexington, KY
12 March 2011